Growing and Reimagining Chaplaincy

How to Start, Form and Support Chaplaincies

Mike Haslam

Chaplaincy Adviser, Di[illegible]th and Wells

GROVE BOOKS LIMITED

RIDLEY HALL RD CAMBRIDGE CB3 9HU

Contents

Foreword by Bishop Ruth Worsley

In the Diocese of Bath and Wells we have seen a recent surge in those called to a role as chaplain; the very young and much older folk have come forward in established chaplaincies and in pioneering contexts. It is exciting to see how God has called people in everyday ways to live and tell the story of God's love for the world. Mike's contribution to this growth and development has been hugely significant and I commend this Grove booklet to all who are keen to find new ways to support people in their faith journey. It may take you to unexpected places!

Acknowledgments

Thank you to the chaplaincies within Somerset and beyond whose stories have contributed to this book, many of them explicitly. Thank you especially to the Diocese of Bath and Wells for creating spaces for chaplaincy to grow. Thank you to my family for all of their support, encouragement and editing.

Church Mission Society supports the Grove Mission and Evangelism Series

At Church Mission Society, we believe that every Christian is called to join in God's mission, whether that means crossing the street or crossing continents, and we want to set people free to put that call into action.

First Impression February 2022

ISSN 2399-6536

ISBN 978 1 78827 221 6

Introduction

1

> 'I think that God may be calling me to be a chaplain.'
> 'Can you help us set up a chaplaincy?'

These are two of the most common things that I hear, and I give thanks to God for them. Organizations and communities that have never before had any explicit spiritual presence are now asking for this, in the form of chaplaincy. At the same time, people of faith are coming forward to serve as chaplains.

Chaplaincy is an ancient ministry. It is said to originate with Martin of Tours (316–397 AD). Martin ripped his army cloak (*capella*) in two and gave half to a beggar. He became known as the first capellainor or chaplain. After ordination, Martin was commissioned to work away from the main church building in places where people were in special need. Buildings created for this special work were known as chapels.

There is a long history of chaplaincy in HM Forces and HM Prisons, in hospitals and in universities. There has been a significant movement of industrial and workplace chaplaincy, which continues in a range of different ways. In recent years, chaplaincy has grown, diversified and flourished, especially where there has been time and focus given to chaplaincy development. Many of us involved in chaplaincy discern the breath of God's Spirit within this growth.

All Church of England priests and deacons, in their Declaration of Assent, speak of the faith which the church is 'called upon to proclaim afresh in each generation.'[1] I believe that the growth of chaplaincy is part of this new expression of faith for our generation, as we live and share the story of God's great love in the public spaces of our world. Chaplaincy is far bigger and more diverse than any one faith, certainly than any single denomination. However, within the Church of England, it fits perfectly within the 2020s' vision of a simpler, humbler, bolder church of younger and more diverse missionary disciples celebrating the mixed ecology of mission and ministry. The vision could almost have been written for chaplaincy and it certainly gives chaplaincy space to continue to flourish and be part of the mission narrative.

Chaplaincy has such a diversity of impacts. Students encountering faith through their chaplain and asking to be baptized. Head teachers recognizing and giving thanks for the listening ear, the sympathetic word, the peace and the quiet but constant flicker of hope.[2] Teenagers finding that they can live out their faith more fully in school, because of the chaplain.

Within the context of COVID a nurse said that:

> Chaplaincy helps us support the patients. The chaplains have taught me a lot about speaking to patients, how to be calm with them. They are excellent with patients. Chaplaincy has helped us staff as well, especially me. I am a member of the BAME community. I did struggle, I was very scared. The chaplain came and spent time and spoke to me and made me feel a bit better, made me feel I wasn't on my own.[3]

A member of staff at Hinkley Point C Nuclear Power Station said that the new chaplaincy is 'very helpful professionally and personally [coming from a place of extreme scepticism]. The chaplain draws people together across boundaries. The impact can't be described in numbers.'[4] That impact is also experienced by chaplains who continue to learn and grow within their ministry.

There is such potential to enrich and transform individuals, organizations and communities through chaplaincy.

A Personal Note in a Wider Context

There are as many models of chaplaincy as there are of the local church. Chaplaincy is diverse and ecumenical, multifaceted and multi-faith. In part this is because it is so deeply rooted in diverse and multifaceted communities.

My own experience is as an ordained Anglican chaplain within education and parish contexts, and then as leader of a network of over 150 chaplaincies of all sectors, contexts and traditions across Somerset. In this Grove booklet I will remain aware of the wider context, but I will focus on chaplaincy as I understand and experience it from a Christian perspective within Somerset and beyond.

I am profoundly grateful to each of the chaplaincies within Somerset, whose stories have contributed to this book, many of them explicitly. However, I am writing in my own name as I advocate for chaplaincy development and the continuing opportunities and imperative to grow chaplaincy.

Chaplaincy: 'Listen, Care, Pray and Bless'

2

An 11-year-old pupil was asked what the school chaplain did. He replied that the chaplain was there,

> To listen, care, pray for and bless the school.

This remains one of the most all-encompassing and concise definitions I have heard.

Missional and Incarnational

Christian chaplaincy is a missional and incarnational ministry, going out from the local church, meeting people where they are and living and sharing faith there. God is already present in each and every community. Chaplaincy can enable that divine presence to be revealed and articulated anew for each generation. Chaplaincy is present and rooted in communities, offering welcome and accompaniment to all within them, to people of all faiths, cultures and traditions. Chaplains are spiritual leaders in their communities, with a pastoral and prophetic ministry for each individual, from the powerless to the powerful, and for the whole community, developing and nurturing its ethos and values.

Chaplains are members of the team, living within the policies and the culture of the organization and community they serve, experiencing the same joys and challenges as everyone else. Chaplains are also guests in almost every conversation, for chaplaincy is an offer, not an expectation: no one has to talk with a chaplain. We are in the world we serve, right at its heart, listening, caring, praying and nurturing community and ethos. Yet we are not of that world; we are guests on the edge (John 15.19 and John 17.14–16). This is still true when the chaplain is also a member of staff with more than one role within the organization. Even if only a few hours a week are allocated to the chaplaincy role, it will permeate everything; yet it is still distinctive and different to the role of teacher, paramedic, bus driver or pastoral worker.

This missional and incarnational ministry means that we can also be there, and be trusted, when things are tough. When the Taunton Debenhams closed, the chaplain was a familiar face, valued and respected for her long service to the store. The staff trusted her as an independent voice and were able to talk to her of their fears and grief. She created safe spaces for reflection, fellowship and prayer and continued to serve the store and the staff up to its closure and beyond.

In a different way, at the start of the COVID lockdown in the spring of 2020 the chaplain at Hinkley Point C was told by a senior member of staff, 'If you leave site we're f***ing stuffed.' Another member of staff put it slightly differently when he said to the chaplain, 'Thanks for making us feel safe, mate.' The chaplain reflected that 'Presence is such a huge part of chaplaincy and a little bit goes a long way. Maybe that is because we represent a bigger presence.'[5]

This sense of presence has also been noticed within education. The Vice Principal of an FE college commented, 'We didn't realize how much value the chaplain gave until he wasn't there.'[6] The college have since appointed a new chaplain. Soon after appointing a chaplain for the first time, the head teacher of a community school wrote, 'The chaplain has contributed so much to our community as a non-church school. I suspect that there have been benefits for us that we had perhaps not expected. He has earned huge respect in our community and added a calming and reflective element to our culture, which is noticeable when he is with us.'[7]

In an acute context, a ward sister at Royal United Hospitals Bath NHS Foundation Trust said after the first COVID lockdown, 'I wouldn't have got through the last few months without the chaplains. The support they gave the staff and patients through a very difficult time was amazing. They've got this knack of finding you, this inner sense of where you are and when you need them to visit.'[8]

Chaplains are there to create safe spaces to explore questions of life and faith

Chaplains do not jump in to join the dots, or explain what it is about chaplaincy presence that enables people to find healing and safety and peace, or where the inner sense comes from. Yet chaplains are there to respond to the questions when they are asked and to create safe spaces to explore questions of life and faith. To return to Hinkley Point C, one member of staff said that the chaplain's open, welcoming presence on site had drawn him to ask questions that he had been avoiding for years, and find faith.

Sanctuary

One aspect of the presence of chaplaincy is the offer of safe space. This can be a physical space, such as a chaplaincy room, a spiritual care centre or a chapel. Such a space can have advantages and offer a haven and sanctuary where people can gather, pray, breathe and be still. However, these spaces do also need to be managed and supervised. In a school context, for instance, a chaplain can have a group of vulnerable students gathering in a chaplaincy space and that is hugely valuable. Yet that also means that the chaplain is not as present across the rest of the school, in the hall, canteen or playing fields. The ministry risks becoming attractional, seeking to draw people in, rather than missional, going out to be with people. Whether or not there is a physical space, chaplains create safe space wherever they are, in reception or office, café or pub, corridor or by the water-cooler. Such spaces could be considered as the equivalent of Jacob's well at which Jesus met the Samaritan woman in John 4.

A Kingdom Ministry

Chaplaincy is a kingdom ministry. Whilst doing Christmas shopping I met a former pupil who told me with enormous pride that he was now at university, the first member of his family to become an undergraduate. He said that I was one of the people who helped him believe that he could achieve such a goal. That particular pupil was one of the hundreds for whom I worked with the local food bank to offer holiday meals to those who needed them. It is for the same reasons that chaplains support those living with mental ill-health and poverty and any kind of crisis.

Dr Mike Osborn, Consultant Macmillan Clinical Psychologist at Royal United Hospitals Bath NHS Foundation Trust, said of chaplaincy:

> Acute hospitals are very hot, busy places. It's a challenge to meet the targets and offer therapeutic care. Chaplains are essential. They are present in every part of the hospital, offering spiritual and psychological care. Without them, who else is there, offering that level of contact and comfort? Without the chaplaincy we would continue to focus on the bio-medical data but we would be at risk of losing touch with the real, lived experience of patients.
>
> Medics are under pressure to be concise and knowing. At the heart of chaplaincy is uncertainty, unknowing, journeying with people. The chaplain's main therapeutic 'weapon' is powerlessness.
>
> Chaplains have an overview of the whole hospital and an independence. They speak truth to power in a helpful and constructive way. They offer intimate support to patients and are a critical friend to the organization. They both 'rise above it' and get mucky and involved.
>
> The chaplaincy gift of time and listening is as important as sterile conditions in a hospital operating theatre. Time is their infection-control measure. If chaplaincy didn't exist, you'd have to invent it pretty fast.[9]

Courageous advocacy is another aspect of chaplaincy kingdom ministry and it is a key feature of port chaplaincy. As much as 95% of all that we import into the UK comes to us by sea. Those who sail our ships are therefore vital to our lives and they need our care.

The chaplain is the only person who is not there to inspect or demand something

When a seafarer has not been paid for months, is overworked or bullied, has not been fully trained or is sailing in a ship that is unsafe, the fact that a chaplain stands up for them brings hope to their situation. Whilst the chaplain has no direct power, pastoral visits may be the point at which a serious situation is uncovered. The chaplain then involves the port authorities, the International Transport Federation, the Merchant Navy Welfare Board and others who have the power to improve things. The chaplain is the only person visiting a ship who is not there to inspect or demand something. Real hope lies in the chaplain's visits.

Can Anyone be Forgiven?

Within this kingdom context, chaplains are both distinctive and inclusive. I do not believe that there is any point in being so woolly that no one knows what we believe; I am a Christian, a Jesus person, and I will share my faith at any appropriate opportunity. However, just as importantly, chaplains are there to welcome everyone, unconditionally, whatever their beliefs, culture or context. To do this, chaplains need to face cultural perceptions that the church will judge you or only accept you if you are good enough and fit a stereotype. Such perceptions can only be overcome through patience, prayer and the slow, steady building of relationships and trust. Chaplains invest and give this time and build the relationships with their communities. Healthcare chaplains speak of being 'patient-led': they are as ready to listen to a patient talk of their garden as of their beliefs. This is about meeting people where they are, on their turf, in their time, rather than expecting them to come to us and conform to our standards and expectations.

This applies even when we are greeted with a profound question of faith and life, as I was when a patient called me to his hospital bedside and asked me, 'Can anyone be forgiven?' My first response was not to share my faith in God's love and mercy, but to ask him, 'What do you think?' I wanted to know if he was thinking of himself, or of someone who might have hurt him, if he had a background of faith or was starting to explore for the first time, if he was asking because he was scared of death, or if this was a long-standing question. By seeking to meet him where he was on that day, in that place, I was able to have a conversation that I hope meant something to him and enabled him to understand a bit more about forgiveness.

Walking Slowly

As Christian chaplains, our ministry is rooted in the example of Jesus: being present, noticing those in need, welcoming everyone without condition and journeying alongside them. I was once waiting to interview a candidate for the post of lead hospital chaplain. The person concerned was already a member of the chaplaincy team and was at work that day. She was about 20 minutes late for the interview because of the number of people who had asked to talk to her as she walked from one side of the hospital to the other. To each she had given presence and time and care, with a sense that this was where God needed her to be at this particular moment. This was far more important than a small matter of timing and we appointed her as lead chaplain.

Another colleague, a chaplain in a large secondary school, noticed that almost everyone on campus was over-busy, pressured and rushing. In response, she decided to walk slowly and prayerfully, to be present in each moment and to try to notice those who might need help, so that she could in turn respond.

In the ministry of these two chaplains, and that of so many others, I sense something of the encounter of Jesus and Zacchaeus. If Jesus was not walking slowly, prayerfully alert to notice his surroundings, how could he have seen the little man in the sycamore tree amidst all of the crowds of Jericho? Jesus had many competing demands in this period in Luke's gospel, welcoming the children, healing the sick, teaching his disciples, challenging the rulers and the encroaching crowds as he drew closer to Jerusalem. Yet he still noticed and welcomed Zacchaeus, the hated tax collector, and blessed him with his presence. We do not hear anything that Jesus said to Zacchaeus about his way of life, but something about the encounter transformed Zacchaeus' life and we do hear Christ's words of thanks that 'salvation has come to this house' (Luke 19.1–10).

If Jesus was not walking slowly, how could he have seen Zacchaeus?

I was recently listening to a university student who saw in the chaplaincy a space where people of different backgrounds, contexts and cultures were welcome. He said, 'I've connected with other people and formed friendships through the chaplaincy, with people I wouldn't normally spend time with.' He went on to say that he had met with the chaplain and explored Scripture and questions of life and faith. He had joined in daily prayers through the COVID lockdowns. This is a part of the story of Jesus and Zacchaeus that we can only imagine. Yet the end of the student's story echoes that of Zacchaeus. He said, 'The chaplaincy gave me hope that Christianity could be for me. They gave me a vision of the church family, before I'd met the church.'[10]

Faith at Work

Through being present as a person of faith and creating spaces for fellowship, prayer and learning, chaplaincy enables the people of faith who are already present in the community to grow in their understanding of how to live out their discipleship in the workplace. Once again, this is not about imposition or assumption. Instead, chaplains notice the people of faith, listen and care, and offer opportunities for prayer, fellowship and exploration where all are welcome. As a result, chaplaincy has been a seedbed for vocation within the church. Many who are coming forward for lay and ordained ministry have a part of their faith journey in chaplaincy.

The 95%

In every aspect of chaplaincy ministry and mission, chaplains are there with the 95% who do not have regular (monthly) contact with a local church.[11] Chaplains are there in workspaces and places of learning and healing, they are there with cultural networks and dispersed and marginalized communities. Chaplains are not waiting for people to come to them, they are there alongside, there with an offer rather than an expectation, there to listen, care, pray and bless.

Mohammed is a Syrian refugee. He has lived in the UK for two years and is now in Year 6 of primary school. When I met with him he said of his school chaplain:

> When I was in Year 4 she helped me a lot. When I was angry, she helped. She had a big bear in her room; afterwards, I felt happy.

Later in the same conversation, when I asked about collective worship, Mohammed said:

> She does interesting stuff about Jesus. I'm a Muslim, I'm still interested.

This deep level of trust, conveyed even through a second language, is rooted in the fact that the chaplain had given this young refugee such care and time and compassion. She also spoke to me about how, when Mohammed decided to keep the Ramadan fast for the first time, she supported him and gave him space to talk about this in collective worship and they explored fasting in the Abrahamic faiths.[12]

3

Developing Chaplaincy: Imperative and Opportunity

Most weeks I hear from people asking if God is calling them to be a chaplain. Most months I hear from organizations and communities asking how to create a chaplaincy. These wonderful questions are also heard by my colleagues who are involved in developing chaplaincy within and beyond Somerset. As I write this Grove booklet there are six new chaplaincies in development and another three which have just been launched. Chaplaincy is a growing part of the mixed ecology of the church.

Despite amazing exceptions, the general picture of church membership continues to be one of decline. In this context, it is good news to hear that secular organizations, who have never before experienced any explicit spiritual ministry, would like a chaplain. These requests for chaplaincy are missional opportunities to journey alongside the 95% who do not have regular (monthly) contact with a local church. Such opportunities cannot be ignored. Of course, chaplains are not the only ministry working with the 95%. Baptisms, weddings and funerals, church schools, youth and children's ministry, food banks, street pastors, pioneering, community cafés, church festivals and other ministries all offer opportunities for engagement. Alongside our local churches, these expressions of faith are crucial parts of our reimagining of our ministry and mission.

It has long been noted that not all community or identity is geographical, and with each passing year the diversity of spaces in which we find our identity and our sense of home grows. Yet one of the defining and most valued features of the local church is that it is locally based. Chaplaincy is one of the ministries which reaches beyond geography. It is present in workplaces and leisure, for instance, in sports and the arts, in places of learning and in dispersed cultural communities, such as travellers. This is another aspect of chaplaincy meeting people where they are, at work, learning or leisure, rather than trying to connect with them in residential communities where they may do little more than sleep.

Growing Chaplaincy

Depending quite how you count and define a chaplaincy, around fifty chaplaincies have been created in Somerset over the past five years.[13] This has not just happened. Growth has occurred where churches have established regional or diocesan chaplaincy development, as the Diocese of Bath and Wells has. Below are a few examples of this growth.

School Chaplaincy

8.45pm on a school day is not the best of times to present a new idea to a head teacher, yet that was when I was scheduled to address a diocesan gathering of head teachers and multi-academy trust chief executives. I had a ten-minute slot before closing prayers and shared a day in the life of a chaplain. Five of the community schools present asked me to work with them to create chaplaincies for the first time. All those chaplaincies now exist. The chaplains are present to live and share faith with thousands of students and staff. One of the newly appointed chaplains has gone on to set up a chaplaincy to another community secondary school. Another, appointed for two days a week and funded by the local churches, was, within a year, offered an additional two days per week, funded by the school. She works with over eighty students at any one time. Chaplaincy is now considered by that school to be essential, invaluable and irreplaceable.

Court Chaplaincy

When I visited the Magistrates' Court at Weston-super-Mare to discuss the creation of a new chaplaincy there, my conversation with the chief usher opened with these words.

> 'I'm here to ask if you'd be interested in chaplaincy.'
> 'Of course we are. When can you start, tomorrow?'

A classic scenario in which the chaplain could help might be as follows. A young man is sentenced to a prison sentence. His family is left distraught; their life has been torn apart. Despite their desire to help, the ushers have a responsibility to get the next case into court. The chaplain has a precious gift of time and can be there to listen and care. There are times when the young man happens to have the car keys in his pocket; the chaplain can help to retrieve those, so that the family can return home. They might have lost a crucial income, and the chaplain can offer food-bank vouchers and signpost to financial support and advice. The chaplain can also find out which prison the man has been sent to and let the family know how to make contact.

Sadly, the court chaplaincy start date has been delayed by COVID, but the Taunton team has just started and the Weston-super-Mare team is nearly ready to begin.

YMCA Chaplaincy

The chaplain to a YMCA centre had resigned and the YMCA CEO asked to meet with me. I thought that the meeting was about appointing a new chaplain. Instead, I was asked to significantly expand chaplaincy and create a network of chaplains for each of the sixteen centres within the YMCA.

Those chaplains offer regular care and prayer to young people and staff. One of them, chaplain to a centre set up for the homeless during COVID, gained such trust from one resident, that he told her he could not read. The chaplain, a retired teacher, offered to teach him and in due course he invited friends to the informal lessons, which became so big that they were eventually taken on by a local further education college.

Emergency Service Chaplaincy

Support was given to Devon and Somerset Fire and Rescue Service, who have recently appointed chaplains. Then South Western Ambulance Service asked for help to establish chaplaincy and spiritual care. Conversations which began with exploration of chaplaincy as one of many options and priorities have become committed, and we are close to being able to appoint.

Anna Chaplaincy

Anna Chaplaincy offers spiritual care to those in the latter years of life, people in care homes and in the community. The ministry is growing in Somerset as it is across the UK. In Somerset we are also working with other hospice chaplains, care home chaplains and the NHS to enable everyone to have an offer of spiritual care at the end of life.

Finance

For those who are concerned about the bottom line, finance is as diverse as any other aspect of chaplaincy. Churches have an important role in offering seedcorn funding and there are some chaplaincies that continue to be funded by the churches. However, the overwhelming majority of chaplaincies are funded by organizations, charities, trust funds and local groups. Other chaplaincies are voluntary. Within Somerset, there are 150 chaplaincies and over 300 chaplains (full time and part time). Around 100 of those chaplains are paid. The Diocese of Bath and Wells funds the equivalent of 2.6 full-time posts (including the full-time chaplaincy adviser); Churches Together groups fund the equivalent of 1.4 full-time posts; the rest of the paid posts are externally funded. The equivalent of 7.6 full-time posts have been funded in the last four years as a result of investment in chaplaincy development. This significant and growing investment in spiritual care from a wide range of organizations and trust funds, many of whom have no explicit faith foundation, is testimony to the impact that chaplaincy has. There is continued space for growth.

Advocacy and Impact

I believe that the growth of chaplaincy in Somerset, and in so many other places, is happening by the grace of God. However, if there is one thing that that we have done to help chaplaincy grow, I believe it is advocacy. We have sought to bring chaplaincy from the edge to the centre, at least a little bit, and to make it known as a part of the church's mixed ecology. We have shared stories about chaplaincy and the difference it makes to individuals and communities. We have used every media and platform available, new and old, for this storytelling and advocacy. We have been actively present for meetings, conferences and forums for sectors where there could be chaplaincy development. We have dared to asked the question, 'Would you like to create a chaplaincy?' We have told the story of what chaplaincy offers and the difference it makes. We have also been present in church, in worship and prayer and fellowship, in meetings, synods, working parties and councils. Chaplaincy is part of the church and we have shared our story whenever possible. We have developed toolkits and pathways and offered time and advice that can guide and enable this growth in new chaplaincies.

Chaplaincy is part of the church and we have shared our story whenever possible

From this advocacy of the impact of chaplaincy, by God's grace, have come the new chaplaincies (a few of which are detailed above) and new chaplains. People exploring chaplaincy have come from all denominations and church traditions. They are young and old, ordained and lay, from the edge and centre of the church, some with many years of discipleship and ministry behind them and some just beginning their journey of faith. If they have anything in common, it is perhaps a desire to be pastors to people beyond church, to be with them where they are and live and share faith there.

For me, at a sports chaplaincy conference I was asked for my greatest sporting moment. I said that I did not have one (there were gasps of horror!) but that I was there because I was passionate about chaplaincy, meeting people where they are and offering to journey with them. I later reflected that even chaplaincy is only incidental to me, although it seems to be where God is calling me. I am passionate about working alongside the 95% who do not regularly visit a local church, and chaplaincy is one of the pathways that can enable this ministry and mission.

Just as time, listening and relationship building have been key in developing chaplaincy with organizations, so they are essential in helping people of faith to discern their vocation to chaplaincy. Yet without the original advocacy, the storytelling of chaplaincy and its impact, how could many have heard of the option or good news of chaplaincy?

4 Models of Chaplaincy

As has already been stated, there are as many models of chaplaincy as there are of the local church. Chaplaincy can be full time and part time, paid and honorary, in a huge range of sectors, organizations and communities. Chaplains can work alone or as part of large teams. Chaplains can be full-time members of the senior leadership or offer a few hours a week as a volunteer. Chaplaincies, like local churches in all of their ecumenical glory, cover the range of theological traditions and denominations, from evangelical to liberal to catholic and everything in between.

Some chaplains serve within Christian foundations, although in some of these the Christian foundations are deeply buried and part of the chaplaincy role is excavation. Some chaplains serve within entirely secular contexts and some within vibrantly multi-faith communities. Occasionally there is a statutory role for chaplaincy (for instance within HM Prisons or HM Forces), but more often there is a continuing need to demonstrate value and impact so as to justify the role and its funding. Sometimes the language and ethos of spiritual care is used rather than the term 'chaplaincy.'

Since each sector and each community is distinctive, each chaplaincy is also distinctive, speaking the language of their community. Yet despite the diversity and the occasional temptation to define a chaplaincy or chaplaincy sector by its difference from others, there is far more in the ethos and value of chaplaincy that is held in common than divides. There is certainly no one single best model of chaplaincy. Each enriches the other and can learn from their neighbours. However, a few models of chaplaincy are offered below, with a focus on organizational structure.

Chaplaincy Hubs

Over the past ten years, Taunton Team Chaplaincy (TTC) has developed to a place where it is an established ecumenical Christian charity with a lead chaplain (paid 4 days per week) leading a team of 36 honorary chaplains. The honorary chaplains are all members of local churches and give between half a day and one day a week. They serve across a number of clusters:

- Retail
- Offices

- Care homes
- Rail responders
- Parks and gardens (open spaces)
- Marginalized (homeless)
- Magistrates' Court

Each cluster has a convener. Chaplains meet for learning, prayer and fellowship in clusters and as a whole team. TTC is financed by local churches and trust funds. TTC has grown in partnership with local churches, Street Pastors and a wide range of civic and community groups and organizations. It has a significant reputation in the community and receives as many, if not more, requests for chaplaincy as it can staff with its amazing team of volunteers. Recent requests for chaplaincy have come from the Magistrates' Court and from a hostel for the homeless, which was set up at the start of lockdown in Spring 2020.

In 2019 (before COVID) the chaplains within the Taunton Team had 5,000 reported significant encounters with people. These conversations were broken down as follows.

Encounters	Number of Encounters
Prayer offered	400
Faith (theirs or the chaplains) discussed	1050
Work (they shared something important)	1150
Family and relationships (they shared something important)	800
Health (they shared something important)	350
Signposted to another agency	50
Community engagement (Lead Chaplain)	700
Other	500

This model of a paid lead chaplain, who calls, trains and supports a team of volunteers, is echoed in many contexts, such as the police, education and health care.

Honorary Chaplaincy

There are also situations where chaplaincy is entirely honorary. Examples of this include chaplaincy to an agricultural market, chaplaincy to Devon and Somerset Fire and Rescue Service and village chaplaincy.

One example of honorary village chaplaincy can be found in West Buckland in Somerset. It is a community with a population of about 1000, just off the M5. It is part of a large team ministry and Tracey Richbell, the village chaplain, who is also a churchwarden, is a key leader of the local church. She was commissioned at the very start of lockdown in spring 2020. She put on her walking boots and took to the streets. She is there to listen to people on their doorsteps, on their daily walks and in their farmyards. People who were not members of the church, people who were, and people who were exploring faith all responded to the question, 'What difference does chaplaincy make?' and offered the following thoughts:

- We need chaplains, a friend coming into your lives, knowing the challenges.
- Chaplaincy is wonderful and non-judgmental.
- The chaplain opens doors to faith and church.
- The chaplain enables us to be more in touch with the church, even though we don't go.
- The chaplain has opened the door and got the congregation going again.
- The chaplain is on the ground, giving time, giving love.
- The chaplain is a leader in the church and the village who is known by many.
- Faith is coming back slowly and I'm becoming part of the church family, because of the chaplain.

Chaplaincy as Part of Local Church Ministry

There are school chaplains who fulfil the role within a wider youth and children's ministry, employed by the local church. One such chaplain, an outstanding children and families' worker with many years of valued ministry in the local church, school and community found that, when she was formally appointed primary school chaplain, the impact of the hours she spent in the school suddenly increased. Her hours in the school remained roughly the same, but there was a new level of trust, from staff, children and parents. People were asking her questions about her faith for the first time and there were also new opportunities to offer practical and pastoral care. This model of chaplaincy can also be lived out through an ordained church leader, who might be chaplain to a local YMCA centre, football club, community hospital or FE college.

Full-time Paid Chaplaincy

There is a long history of full-time paid chaplains in hospitals, schools, universities, industrial sites, HM Prisons and HM Forces. Sometimes these chaplaincies involve teams of paid chaplains and staff, interns and volunteers. Within Somerset, nearly all of the chaplaincies created in 2017–2022 have been part time; although on occasion, a number of part-time roles have been combined into one full-time chaplaincy, perhaps resembling the structure of a multi-parish benefice.

However, the Hinkley Point C Nuclear Power Station Chaplaincy was an example of new full-time paid chaplaincy. There are around 6,000 workers on site at any one time, and over the period of the build 25,000 people will have been employed there. The workforce is significantly younger and more diverse than many church congregations. There is also a large cohort of young men, working away from home. For all of these reasons, both the Somerset church leaders and Hinkley Point C judged that it was important to create and fund a full-time chaplaincy post.

Creating Chaplaincy

5

Bilingual Expectations

Chaplaincies are bilingual places. Chaplains need to be able to speak the languages both of their faith communities and of the organizations within which they minister. In the same way, the creation of a chaplaincy is a bilingual process.

When a chaplaincy is envisaged and planned there can be many mixed motives, from every side. There can also be confusion because of widespread misunderstandings of chaplaincy, within and beyond the church. From an organizational perspective, there may be hopes that chaplains will be stand-in mental health first-aiders or additional pastoral workers who will address and resolve challenging situations. Churches may hope that a chaplaincy can bring new people into Sunday worship, *Alpha* or the youth group, or can reduce levels of guilt that a church is not connecting with an FE college, police station or traveller site in the parish.

It is therefore essential that there is clear communication, even and especially if it takes place in more than one language, and with more than one set of expectations.

Seedcorn

The offering of seedcorn funding from the churches is important in the creation of chaplaincy. This initial funding can come in different forms, in kind and in cash. However, whatever the form, it is an opportunity for churches to demonstrate the value and impact of chaplaincy to a new organization.

Hinkley Point C Nuclear Power Station were interested in chaplaincy, but not yet committed. As a part of the development process, an Anglican rector and Methodist minister each offered them a day of chaplaincy per week for six months. This was time that the two ordained leaders were able to give out of their existing ministries. Hinkley were so impressed that they agreed to appoint and pay a full-time chaplain. However, Hinkley were keen to maintain the partnership nature of the post, so they asked the Diocese of Bath and Wells to be the employer.

There is an increasingly long list of secondary school chaplaincies that were started with funding from church groups or charities and moved to being funded by the school. There are also chaplains in a wide range of contexts who have started in an honorary role and then begun to be paid by the organizations they serve.

Creating a Partnership

At its best, chaplaincy is a partnership between the local faith communities and the organization or community served. The initiative and vision to create a new chaplaincy can, and does, come from either partner. To become a reality, that initiative needs to include wide-ranging conversations covering the following matters.

Prayer

All we do is by the grace of God and therefore needs to be founded in prayer.

Vision

What is your vision for the chaplaincy? Who are you seeking to serve, and how? How does the spiritual care and leadership element of chaplaincy connect with the pastoral care and mental health first-aid?

Team

Is there a team or working party in place, or one which could be formed, to develop the chaplaincy? Does this represent the different partners involved?

Job or Role Description

How will the vision be translated into a role or job description?

Agreement

Who needs to agree to the creation of the role and the final paperwork? This might be church leadership teams or councils or leadership teams, governors or trustees in organizations. Human resources and finance teams will almost certainly also need to be consulted. It is worth planning a timetable of the various meeting dates so that the process can run as smoothly as possible.

Employer

Who will be the employer? If the funding is coming from or via a small charity which does not have any paid employees, it can be helpful for the organization that the chaplaincy will be serving to take on the employment and payroll responsibilities.

Finance

Will the new chaplaincy be honorary or paid? If it is paid, what will be the hours, salary and on-costs? If it is honorary there still needs to be a budget to pay for training and expenses. Where will the funding come from and how will it be sustained?

Safeguarding and Statutory Responsibilities

Who will be responsible for safer recruitment and the DBS and safeguarding process? Who will be responsible for insurance and other statutory responsibilities?

Recruitment

What is the recruitment process and timetable and who will be involved? If it is an honorary post with a clear candidate, it may not be necessary or appropriate to advertise, but a safer-recruitment process is still essential. This is not only about safeguarding. Such a process helps to clarify the vision and mutual expectations and ensure that they are shared by all involved.

Line Management, Supervision and Support

Who will be the line manager? Will that role be held by someone in the church or in the organization? It can also be appropriate to appoint a supervisor to work alongside the line manager to represent the other partner. Ideally the chaplain will meet regularly with representatives of their organization and the church community. This meeting offers support to the chaplain and ensures that all partners continue to share a common vision for the chaplaincy. It also helps to identify and resolve any difficulties at an early stage. A support group can also be appropriate.

Induction, Training and Mentoring

How will you induct the chaplain? What initial and ongoing training is appropriate? An offer of mentoring can be part of this.

Commissioning

Do you hope to begin the ministry with a commissioning service and prayer? Whilst this is common in church circles, in almost every other context the public celebration and party comes at the end of role, not at the start. The role of a service of prayer and commissioning will thus need to be explained.

Space and Communications

Will the chaplain have an organizational email and access to the IT system? If not, how will communication work? Will there be a chaplaincy space? (For further reflections on this, see chapter two.)

Uniform

Some kind of identification of the chaplain can be helpful. This will vary depending on the context, from a badge to a shirt, a fleece or a hoodie or even something like a prayer shawl. It can often include the chaplain's name and the organizational logo.

Name

What will the chaplain be called? Again this will vary depending on the context, but clarity on whether the chaplain is called by their first name or their title (in a school) is a part of the development of the vision for the post.

Lay and Ordained

One of the wonderful things about chaplaincy is that almost all posts are open to lay and ordained people. However, there may be times when the role is clearly one for an ordained leader. If this is the case then it needs to be clearly articulated.

Unrealistic Expectations

It is worth addressing any such expectations (for example, that the chaplain will fill the church, or be a stand-in mental-health worker), so that realistic aims and objectives can be agreed.

Prayer, Support and Review

There is a need to continue to support the chaplaincy. A need to continue to pray, to nurture the partnership and support the chaplain, and to review the chaplaincy at key milestones.

Despite the value given to chaplaincy, it will almost always be one of a multitude of matters in a leader's in-box. This is often true both for church and for organizational leaders. There is therefore a role for those leading the development of chaplaincy to prompt the relevant leaders at appropriate stages to ensure that the process runs smoothly.

6

Formation and Support

The Need for Formation and Support

'I'm worried that I'm going to be lonely,' a chaplain said a few weeks before the start of their first chaplaincy post. In what was not my most empathetic or encouraging moment, my first response was, 'Don't worry, you'll certainly be lonely.' The conversation did continue with more empathy, or at least, I hope it did.

Chaplaincy is a lonely ministry. A chaplain will often be in a team of one. There may be a team of volunteers, but they might be very part-time. Even if there is a larger team within a hospital, prison or university, the chaplains will still be a tiny proportion of the overall staff team. Chaplains may well be the only people who are out in public as people of faith, with the keen awareness of their spiritual role and of being in the world and yet not of the world.

Since chaplaincy is there for the whole organization and community it does not sit particularly easily within any individual team. A chaplain may be line managed by the governor, chief executive or head teacher, but is not always a member of the senior leadership team, or any team. Chaplaincy has input into every team. One school chaplain discovered that she was not invited to any of the staff Christmas parties, because although she worked with every team and department, she was not a full member of any of them. There can also be a disconnect from the local and regional faith community, which does not always offer the support or engagement to chaplains that it does to other forms of ministry.

When combined with the limited understanding of chaplaincy, this can lead to the loneliness of chaplaincy; this is despite the strong support of so many organizations, communities and churches. Therefore, there is a need for specialist chaplaincy development support, for those who are exploring chaplaincy and for those serving within it.

Just as there is no one model of chaplaincy, so there is no single model for training, formation or support. The options for chaplaincy training are currently regrettably limited. There is a range of Masters-level courses at universities. There are also chaplaincy modules and placements within other ministerial and theological training courses. Newman University offers a one-year post-graduate certificate in chaplaincy. Various denominations, networks and chaplaincies and chaplaincy sectors offer shorter, informal courses. These include:

- *Exploring Healthcare Chaplaincy:* www.network-health.org.uk/index.php/pages/exploring-healthcare-chaplaincy-course
- *Educational Chaplaincy training:* Centre For Chaplaincy in Education, www.centreforchaplaincyineducation.co.uk
- *Church Mission Society* offers a module on chaplaincy: https://pioneer.churchmissionsociety.org/?s=chaplaincy
- *Newman University Postgraduate Certificate in Chaplaincy:* newman.ac.uk/course/chaplaincy-pgcert/september-2022
- *Methodist Church, Chaplaincy Everywhere:* methodist.org.uk/our-work/our-work-in-britain/chaplaincy/chaplaincy-everywhere

Exploring Chaplaincy

Anyone wanting to explore chaplaincy is encouraged to research local courses. However, as a model of what can be possible, *Exploring Chaplaincy* was developed in the Diocese of Bath and Wells.[14] It is an eight-session introduction to and exploration of chaplaincy. It is relevant to those who are discerning if they are being called to chaplaincy, and to those who have just begun such a ministry. It has been helpful for those with decades of discipleship and ministry and for those just beginning their journey of faith. In its development we were indebted to the Methodist Church's *Chaplaincy Everywhere* and other courses from which we learnt, developed and adapted.[15]

The eight sessions of *Exploring Chaplaincy* are:

Session 1: Values and ethos of chaplaincy; distinctive and inclusive presence: exploring the qualities of chaplaincy and their theological foundations.

Session 2: Wells: reflecting on Jesus and the woman at the well in John 4, and exploring the wells at which chaplains can meet with people.

Session 3: Listening: revisiting good listening skills, founded on grace.

Session 4: Mental health first aid: using material from Mental Health First Aid UK to inform our response.

Session 5: Prayer and spirituality: reflecting on prayer and spirituality, pastoral and public.

Session 6: Rethinking resilience: reflecting on Paul's letter, 2 Corinthians.

Session 7: Reflective practice and peer supervision: modelling reflective practice.

Session 8: Next steps.

Chaplaincy visit and meeting: A visit to a chaplaincy of your choice can be arranged individually. We also offer a one-to-one conversation to explore vocation and next steps.

Exploring Chaplaincy is run three times a year. In 2021 sixty-two people completed the course, about half from Somerset, the rest from across the UK and as far afield as Austria, India and Zambia. Feedback on the course included:

'Thank you to you for increasing my awareness and helping me to grow spiritually, as I continue on this journey that God has set before me. The openness, sincerity and faith will be a part of my building blocks in going forward.'

'I've found *Exploring Chaplaincy* so helpful personally but also empowering in so many ways; I know I shall be able to be a better chaplain for having done the course. After a long day, training can feel a step too far, but it has been such a blessing to meet and hear from others and to reflect after each session.'

The feedback, the number of people on the course and the geographical diversity all speak of the need for such courses. *Exploring Chaplaincy* and similar courses are just a beginning; do look for one in your area.

Placements and Reflection

Within or beyond a course, whether formal or informal, long term or short term, a placement can be an invaluable means of discerning a calling to chaplaincy. Anyone can search for a chaplaincy—get in touch and ask for a placement. However, the presence and involvement of those charged with chaplaincy development can mean that the offers can be made, the dots can be connected and the placements set up. A placement ceases to be an exception and becomes the norm. Chaplaincy development can also offer informed and reflective conversations on vocation. Too often, people exploring chaplaincy are reflecting on it with church leaders who have little direct experience or understanding.

Induction and Mentoring

A new chaplain starting in a new chaplaincy will need support to avoid feeling like you have been thrown off a cliff into ice-cold water with a strong current dragging you out to sea and high waves threatening to crash you onto rocks! Chaplaincy development can offer induction and arrange for the relevant training, both within the organization and from the church. A mentor can also be offered for the first year in post so that the new chaplain has an experienced chaplain from outside their organization to reflect with. Even with an experienced chaplain in a new post, the first year can be considerably easier if there is smooth and effective induction and training, and ongoing mentoring.

Review and On-going Training and Fellowship

Just as there are limited options for initial chaplaincy training, so there is a regrettable scarcity of opportunities for on-going training and formation. In Somerset we offer a programme of fellowship, training and prayer, days when everyone gathers, and time for specific chaplaincy sectors or geographical areas. A programme for the year includes:

- Chaplaincy Gathering: a day for everyone, with keynote speakers, workshops, prayer and fellowship.
- Quiet days: spaces for reflection, prayer and fellowship.
- Regular training and gathering for chaplaincy sectors: for instance, mental health first aid for school chaplains, meetings of agricultural chaplains or gatherings in geographical hubs.
- Reflective practice groups for chaplains, and informal spaces to reflect and pray.
- Pastoral and reflective visits from the chaplaincy adviser to chaplaincies.
- Throughout COVID, lead chaplains from different sectors have been meeting regularly with the bishop.

Occasional reviews of each chaplaincy can also be opportunities for the chaplaincy and chaplains to learn and grow, to take stock, to discern impact, to celebrate good news and hear what could be better and to seek the next steps. Individual chaplains can also benefit from such ministry reviews, which may be offered to some ordained chaplains, but rarely to lay chaplains. Again, anyone can initiate and lead a chaplaincy review, but if there is chaplaincy development it can become a normal, healthy expectation that will help chaplaincy and chaplains to continue to learn and grow.

None of this is rocket science; nor is it new. Yet it is remarkably and regrettably uncommon, except when care and attention is given to chaplaincy development. As in any field, effective formation, training and support leads to growth.

7

Conclusion

I hope and pray that you have been excited and inspired by the diverse stories of chaplaincy across Somerset and the impact that chaplaincy has within its communities. Many new chaplaincies start very small, but with support and prayer, they grow and flourish. We still have much to learn in Somerset. There are so many opportunities to grow that all may live life in all its fullness. I hope and pray that you have also been excited and inspired by the idea of chaplaincy development, and its potential to help chaplaincy grow in depth and numbers as part of the mixed ecology of church. Like everything, the growth of chaplaincy is about God, not about us. However, if through chaplaincy development, we can tell the story of chaplaincy and offer models for chaplaincy set-up, vocation, formation and ongoing support, if we can help to create well-tilled soil and space to grow, then amazing things can, and do, happen.

Chaplaincy Reading List

K Murphy and B Whorton, *Chaplaincy in Hospice and Palliative Care* (London: Jessica Kingsley Publishers, 2017)

J Caperon, A Todd and J Walters, *A Christian Theology of Chaplaincy* (London: Jessica Kingsley Publishers, 2018)

M Threlfall-Holmes and M Newitt, *Being a Chaplain* (London: SPCK, 2011)

J Norman, *At the Heart of Education: School Chaplaincy and Pastoral Care* (Dublin: Veritas, 2004)

D O'Malley, *School Ethos and Chaplaincy* (Bolton, MA: Don Bosco, 2008)

J Caperon, *A Vital Ministry: Chaplaincy in Schools in The Post-Christian Era* (London: SCM Press 2015)

V Slater, *Chaplaincy Ministry and the Mission of the Church* (Norwich: SCM Press, 2015)

A Todd, M Cobb and C Swift, *A Handbook of Chaplaincy Studies: Understanding Spiritual Care in Public Places* (Farnham: Ashgate 2015)

M Saunders, *Chaplaincy: A Ministry of Presence* (USA: lulu.com, 2016)

P Nash and N Roberts, *Chaplaincy with Children and Young People* (Grove Youth booklet Y43)

D Tregale, *Fresh Experiences of School Chaplaincy* (Grove Education booklet eD6)

Notes

1 The Church of England, 'The Declaration of Assent': https://www.churchofengland.org/prayer-and-worship/worship-texts-and-resources/common-worship/ministry/declaration-assent

2 Diocese of Bath and Wells, *Chaplaincy and Hope* (October 2021), p 7: https://bathandwells.org.uk/content/pages/documents/chaplaincy-and-hope.pdf

3 Diocese of Bath and Wells, *Chaplaincy and Coronavirus: Discerning Impact* (October 2020), p 18: https://bathandwells.org.uk/content/pages/documents/chaplaincy-in-covid-times.pdf

4 Bath and Wells, *Chaplaincy and Coronavirus*, *ibid*, p 9.

5 Bath and Wells, *Chaplaincy and Hope*, *op cit*, p 13.

6 Diocese of Bath and Wells, *Chaplaincy in Our Own Words*, p 2, (October 2019): https://bathandwells.org.uk/content/pages/documents/chaplaincy-in-our-own-words.pdf

7 Bath and Wells, *Chaplaincy and Coronavirus*, *op cit*, p 15.

8 Bath and Wells, *Chaplaincy and Coronavirus*, *op cit*, p 5.

9 Bath and Wells, *Chaplaincy and Coronavirus*, *op cit*, p 6.

10 Bath and Wells, *Chaplaincy and Hope*, *op cit*, p 13.

11 https://faithsurvey.co.uk/uk-christianity.html

12 Diocese of Bath and Wells, *Chaplaincy and Hope*, *op cit*, pp 5–6.

13 For an equivalent counting challenge, consider parish churches, daughter churches, chapels of ease, church plants and fresh expressions. All can exist within one parish; are they one church, or many? Similarly, a chaplaincy to three schools within a partnership could be one chaplaincy or three, depending on the context.

14 Diocese of Bath and Wells, *Exploring Chaplaincy*: https://bathandwells.org.uk/content/pages/documents/exploring-chaplaincy-general-precis37544648366.pdf

15 The Methodist Church, *Chaplaincy Everywhere* course: https://www.methodist.org.uk/our-work/our-work-in-britain/chaplaincy/chaplaincy-everywhere/chaplaincy-everywhere-course/)